ART workshops FOR children

Hervé Tullet

Φ

CONTENTS

A WORD OF WELCOME FROM
Herve' Tullet

hello !

Over the following pages, I'd like to give you an insight into what happens in my workshops.

I run creative workshops with children all around the world, from Los Angeles to New Delhi, London to Malawi. The workshops first started as small-scale classroom activities, but soon developed into live art sessions, sometimes with hundreds of participants!

I have always refused to run creative sessions where the goal is to make 'nice pictures'. Instead, I have developed my workshops guided by the idea that the art is a means and not an end. Children are masters of creation – they are very intuitive and it is this instinct and their unedited ability to create art that inspires me.

My workshops are based around getting children to channel that intuition and create freely. To achieve this, I might play a game with them, or speed things up or call out a list of vague instructions. In this way, they are distracted from being self-conscious and shed their inhibitions.

I also believe that collective energy and a great group dynamic is a result in itself. Running workshops with multiple participants creates an energy that empowers each artist to do new and unexpected things. When we improvise as a group, we work from a place of freedom, where all mistakes are permissible and there's no such thing as being over the top. By sharing a special moment together, we can enjoy the added bonus of producing a stimulating piece of artwork.

The facilitator of the workshop – the Leader – plays an important role. Like a musical conductor, choreographer or coach, he or she needs to know where they're headed and must lead the participants through the workshops while also freeing them up by encouraging, stimulating, establishing the rhythm and maintaining the tension so that participants can create the unexpected. The Leader's only caveat is to know when to stop, to avoid things becoming over-painted and 'sludgy': to recognize which combinations will undo the beautiful shapes and colours painted. For this reason, the Leader moves around, pointing out the odd empty patch, taking the pressure off another area that's over-saturated, and helping the participants to strike the right balance.

There is no right or wrong in these workshops. You can always transform an overturned pot of paint, or an instruction that isn't followed or (above all!) an unintended splotch into an inspiring result.

Remember, creative energy is greater than creative control.

A WORD OF ADVICE

Before beginning a workshop, here are my tips:

THE LEADER OF THE WORKSHOP
You need to be heard. It's easy-peasy to make a cone out of thick paper and then decorate it. Hey presto, you've got a loudspeaker! A microphone? Why not! My amplifier of choice: a megaphone! The instructions are often deliberately vague to give participants creative freedom — and so that YOU, as the Leader, have space to make your own variations on my workshops. (By the way, I would love to hear any ideas you have!)

MATERIALS
You'll need to prepare everything in advance to avoid wasting any time during the workshop.

Colour
I like using brightly coloured poster paints in a limited palette. It's best to avoid dark shades, especially brown, as they can 'drown out' the other colours. You can still use black, but separately, to start or finish a workshop for example. ● ● ●

When preparing paints, fill one third of a cup or pot per person, and be ready to refill the cups rather than over-filling them at the start. Each cup should have its own paintbrush. Remember to

make it clear that these stay together and must not get mixed up!
Much as I love paints, you've got to watch out for unwanted
splatters! So, think about suitable clothing for everybody.
All the workshops can also be done with felt-tip pens, pencils
and crayons if you wish.

Paper

Ideally, use big rolls of white paper (wide and thick is best).
You can also use rolls of coloured or black paper, kraft paper,
or any other kind. In a more restricted space, use sheets
of paper spread out. Tape the paper down to stop it from moving,
or, if the workshop is outdoors, use stones to stop the paper from
flying away! You may want to use dustsheets underneath the paper
to prevent the floor from getting dirty.

– – – – –→ SPACE

Make sure the space is suitable for the number of participants:
everybody needs to be able to move around the paper easily.
If there's only a small space available, then most of these
workshops can be done with everybody sitting at a table.

MUSIC

When a workshop is well underway and any initial hesitancy has been
overcome, I strongly suggest playing energetic music, or providing
live musical accompaniment, to focus the group dynamic and to give
the workshop a party mood or theatrical feel.

PARTICIPANTS

You don't need to be a particular age or to have any specific
skills to draw a splotch, an eye, a house, a line or a circle –
these workshops are for everybody! I've held them in all sorts of
places: children's nurseries, market squares, museums, worksites,
school playgrounds, railway station concourses, etc. The only thing
limiting the number of participants is the space available: all my
workshops can be run with four to four hundred participants.

Whether you're in charge of a class of students, toddlers at a nursery
school or a group of adults; whether you're hosting a birthday
party or painting a wall in a festive style, get your creative
juices flowing, follow me and be inventive!

Test a workshop out first, try it out again, adapt and experiment.
Keep observing! You'll always find something new and exciting!

A FIELD OF FLOWERS

I've lost count of how many times
I've run this workshop with
participants of all ages, from
toddlers to grown-ups. The great
thing is that it never fails,
because even the splotches and
mistakes we make along the way are
transformed into something useful,
beautiful and life affirming.

GETTING READY

You'll need lots of different poster paint colours, several large rolls of paper and enough space for your artists to move around. Participants are spread out along the rolls of paper, with their own cup of paint and paintbrush. It's a good idea to play music for the second part of the workshop.

THE WORKSHOP
PART ONE

Are you ready? Here we go! I want to see a tiny dot.

Then, straightaway:

Stop! Everybody swap places.

Having got comfortable, children are sometimes reluctant to change places.

Now I want to see a dot that's a <u>little bit bigger</u>.

Swap places.

I want to see a dot that's even bigger. Reach out and make it a bit further away – not just in front of your nose! We've got plenty of room, so use up all the space!

Swap places.

Now I'd like to see a dot that's bigger still ... a lot bigger, and a lot <u>further away</u>.

Little by little, a rhythm is established between the instructions and moving bodies. Keep the pace lively!

Now I'd like to see a circle.

The participants should swap places with each new instruction.

A bigger circle.

And another circle, a lot bigger.

Are you ready? Here we go! I'd like to see the biggest circle in the world!

The colours are starting to mix ...

Wow! That's pretty ... Almost too pretty!

Moving swiftly on:

Everybody stand up. Take your paintbrush, hold it up ... and let it drop!

Then:

Everybody change places. We're going to do it again, one last time.

Just once more, otherwise we might end up throwing paintbrushes for the rest of the workshop!

Listen very carefully. Now it's time to speed things up!

The instructions start flying faster.
(Don't forget to make everybody swap places each time.)

I want to see:
dots on a dot,
dots inside a circle,
dots around a circle,
dots on a circle,
a circle around a splotch,
a circle around a circle.

Little by little the space is filled, there's a rhythm, a choreography is taking shape.
I carry on giving instructions (variations on the dots and circles) until I think the picture is fairly full, but still has a few

spaces left for us to carry on. And that's
when I say:

**Watch out! Now we need to stop, (look) and handle
our picture with care.**

**Right, you have 30 seconds: take a good look and
paint something if you think it will add to the
bigger picture: a dot, a circle, a splotch maybe
even a spiral.**

Stop! Stand up! The dots and circles are FINISHED!

PART TWO

Children often don't want the game to be
over, but, for the next part, we need to
encourage them to look.

**Now we're going to transform this picture
of dots, circles and splotches into ... a field
of flowers!**

**Listen carefully. To create our field of flowers,
just use your eyes: the flowers are already here!
Choose one and paint the stem and leaves that
belong to it.**

I show them how by demonstrating.

**Start by finding a big flower, add what you like
where you like, and now ... it's your turn to play!**

For this part of the workshop, I enjoy
playing music — something energetic to start
with to accompany the exciting transformation
of splotches into a field of flowers, then
calmer for the later stages.

I move around to see what my artists are
doing and to encourage them, finding a space
for each person and showing them different
examples.

Everybody's busy having fun. Then, little
by little, they put down their paintbrushes,
their body language becomes more relaxed,
their faces look proud and happy as they
stare at ... a huge field of flowers!

VARIATIONS

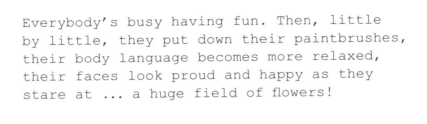

Other work surfaces: you can paint directly
on to walls, fences, even windows!

Different materials: this works just as well
using felt-tip pens, pencils or crayons.

Change elements: the participants can also
try drawing in the dark, or you could ask
a child who has already experienced the
workshop to run it.

THE BIG TRAFFIC JAM

This is perfect to do outside in
a large playground on a sunny day.
By getting lost in the excitement
of 'driving' across the paper with
a paintbrush, participants create
pages full of lively lines from which
we then build a bustling city scene.

GETTING READY

Spread some big rolls of paper on the ground
so that they crisscross. Make sure there is a lot
of space to move around and between the paper.
Lay a series of 'obstacles' evenly across the
paper – old CDs, cones, rocks, sticks, cooking
bowls, plastic cups, boxes, books, shoes –
anything you can get your hands on. You want
as many different shapes as possible. These will
leave empty spaces when removed later.

Every child will need his or her own cup of paint
and brush - use lots of different colours.

THE WORKSHOP

PART ONE

Dip your paintbrush in your paint, find a starting
point on the paper and put your brush there.

Now, imagine your paintbrush is a car taking you
for a ride. Keep it on the paper, watch out for
the obstacles (you mustn't get any paint on them),
and ...

Ready, steady ... go!   !!!!!!!!

Have a nice trip!

Encourage them to move around and travel far.

Hey! Where are you heading? You're going round
in circles. Come on, keep driving! The world's
a big place!

Journeys and children will jostle and overlap
to everybody's amusement.

Some children keep going, some start new
journeys. Lines appear everywhere ...

When the picture is nearly full to bursting,
I ban any new lines.

Stop, end of Part One!

P A R T   T W O

I take away the obstacles.

**Look! The lines you have drawn are actually roads.
Now we've got the roads, let's draw the town.**

Sometimes, I might help them by giving them
specific tips:

We need cars, pedestrians, houses, trees, shops ...

The picture takes on a new life.

The Leader's role is to wander among the
participants, to look, to encourage, to
stimulate, until the picture is out of control
with monstrous traffic jams and sprawling forests.

In order to avoid over-painting and muddying the
picture, paintbrushes are progressively removed,
until there are no more artists in action.

The obstacles are the secret to this workshop's
success: the blank spaces that are left behind,
are now filled with people, cars, trees, etc.

The energy and pleasure of travelling with a
paintbrush is more interesting than a 'pretty'
end product. (Although that's nice too!)

VARIATIONS

Alternative themes: why not draw the sea
using only blue and green for the lines? Then
introduce other colours for the fish, boats and
swimmers. I'm sure there are plenty of other
themes you could imagine? (I'd love to hear
about them!)

THE MAGIC DICE

This is an entertaining dice game that produces endearing monster characters, full of charm and humour. Children love seeing what's unfolding as the game goes on!

GETTING READY

Each artist needs at least one sheet of paper on which a single, large shape has already been drawn (circles, squares, ovals, <u>blops</u> etc.). Find as many dice as there are artists if possible. If not, a single dice works fine! For children under three, use an over-sized dice, spinner or pull numbers out of a hat. The artists work side-by-side, each using a different colour paint or felt-tip pen.

BLOP

THE WORKSHOP

PART ONE

Throw your dice once! The number you throw is the number of eyes you're going to draw in your shape.

I like to make the children swap their pictures at each throw of the dice, but if they want to keep their own drawings, you can suggest swapping colours with a neighbour instead.

Throw your dice a second time! Now you're going to draw that many mouths.

Throw it again! This time, it's for the number of noses.

Now let's throw for how many arms you're going to draw!

And this time it's for the legs!

Ready? Shall we throw again for the ears?

And to finish off, let's draw the hair! Here are my guidelines: 1-2 = a bit of hair, 3-4 = normal, 5-6 = lots of hair.

Now you have a monster!

PART TWO

We've finished with the dice, but let's keep going: Add a background, give your character a name, decorate it and colour it in.

Having created a character, it's time for each artist to invent a whole world and story around it. Where is it? Who are its family and friends? Where does it live? What car does it drive?

Being asked to 'design a character' can be intimidating, but drawing as part of a game helps the participants to shed their inhibitions. And it is often the unexpected combinations that bring the most amazing results!

• • • • VARIATIONS • • • • • • •

Join them up: have the children draw their monsters across a single, large roll of paper. Once the monsters are done, connect the backgrounds to create a monster world!

Change the game: you can assign a shape to each number thrown (1) = eye, (2) = mouth, (3) = nose, (4) = ear, (5) = arm, (6) = leg). Keep throwing the dice until a character has been created from all the shapes. Or you can throw two, three or six dice at a time (why not?)– you might have your monster in one throw!

Work together: the group could create one giant monster together, each participant taking it in turn to add the shape they've 'thrown'.

Maybe you'll make up a new rule? (I'd love to hear about it!)

PAINTING MUSIC

The atmosphere in this workshop positively buzzes. There's a great group dynamic and surprising results as the artists get carried away to music, making colourful splashes, scribbles and marks. The final picture can be magically transformed from abstract pictures into figurative drawings in just a few easy steps.

GETTING READY

Ideally, compile a 20-minute playlist, made up of short, one-minute tracks of music. These can be tuneful or abstract, and very different in register (loud, soft, calm, energetic, contemporary with strange noises, etc.). Even simpler, make music on the spot: find some musicians, or play on your own with two sticks and a pair of maracas to create the rhythms. Or, simplest of all, use your voice. For the second part, prepare some mellow, continuous music.

You'll need to spread out big sheets of different colour paper to fill your space, and have lots of different paint colours. Avoid black and brown for Part One, but have them available for Part Two.

Your artists should stand at the ready, each with his or her paintbrush and a cup of paint.

THE WORKSHOP

 PART ONE

When you hear the music, I want you to react to it on the paper with your paintbrush. When the music changes, swap places.

> If your artists are sitting around a table because of space restrictions, then they can swap their sheets of paper or their brushes when the sound or music stops.
>
> They may feel reluctant, shy or lost to begin with and they might let whole minutes of music go by without doing anything.
>
> Sometimes you really have to push them ...

It might help to close your eyes and react to the sounds. Let yourself be carried away!

Little by little, children join in the rhythm
of the music and the group dynamic takes over.

I wander among the participants, I look,
I remove any sheets of paper that are already
covered in lines and colours to set aside for
Part Two, and I add fresh ones into the mix.

**Stop! Let's stand back and take a look. So what have
we made here?**

Everybody studies the marks, lines and splotches.

We've created a series of backgrounds!

Time to change the soundtrack to something more
mellow and flowing.

**Now we're going to take these backgrounds and
transform them into drawings!**

Symbols or pictograms are great to use here.
They're handy shortcuts that immediately turn
a drawing into a scene.

For example: adding the shape of a simple boat
onto a dynamic blue background makes the boat
look like it's in a storm. Simple cars, trees
and stick-figures are also easy outlines to draw
and, against these backgrounds, they can become
monstrous traffic jams, mysterious forests or
people dancing.

For Part Two, painting with black is often
helpful. Using too many colours on the
paintings can quickly make them over-saturated
or 'muddy', but drawing with black paint or
Indian ink provides definition. Alternatively,
if the paint is thick, I often suggest
intaglio: etching shapes or pictures into the
paint with the handle of the paintbrush.

A PERSONALITY PORTRAIT

I love symbols and pictograms – they
are visual shortcuts that convey an
immediate message, and are easy to
draw. This workshop is about using
a mass of symbols to create a graphic
personality portrait of someone.
The first time I did this workshop
I created the following portrait of the
writer and broadcaster, Michael Rosen.

GETTING READY

Spread some big rolls of paper on the floor or on the wall (this is a group drawing) and put out cups of different colour poster paints, pens and pencils.

Choose a person (or character) whose portrait will be drawn – it needs to be someone everyone is familiar with. Before the workshop, prepare a list of the subject's characteristics together with a selection of possible corresponding signs and pictograms.

Remember, this is a graphic, not a physical representation of your subject, so you can focus on their personality traits, hobbies, job, history etc. and work all sorts of great concepts to do with them into your portrait.

THE WORKSHOP

Talk about your subject to your young portrait artists to get things going. You could even begin to draw as you talk so your artists are relaxed and engaged.

OK, so he's nice: so for that, let's draw a smile.

Now change places.

The participants need to swap places or paintbrushes with each new instruction.

He's chatty: let's draw some letters.
    (Change places)
Is he smart? Hmm, I'm not sure ... How about we draw a question mark?
    (Keep changing places)
He's famous: let's draw a star!
He's messy! What shall we draw? A squiggle?
He's warm: what about a sun?

He likes to dream: let's draw some closed eyes.

Actually, no, he's not nice: cross out that smile.
Ah yes, he's always excited: lightning!
He likes music: a musical note.

He's a king: let's draw a crown.
He's poetic: how about a moon?
He's playful: throw your paintbrush on to the paper!
Hey, he's nice after all: go on, draw a big smile.

He's shy: let's draw a tiny dot.
He's really friendly: let's draw a heart.

By the time the paper is filled, you'll have
a collective drawing that is a very unusual
portrait of someone. One that is beautiful
and full of interpretation and meaning!

∨∨∨∨ VARIATIONS SSSSS

Of course, now you've seen how one portrait
might work, you can translate words into
images in your own way and also encourage
participants to create their own pictographic
dictionary of characteristics. Here are a few
more suggestions to get you started:

joyful (firework)
tidy (square)
intelligent (spiral)
weird (odd shape)
boring (a straight, 'boring' line)

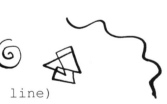

PORTRAIT OF A WORD

This is a variation involving letters as well
as symbols. I choose a word in advance and
work out detailed instructions so that I don't
reveal the word until the end. Participants
fill their paper with shapes and letters one

after another according to my instructions
until the word magically appears!

This is a nice variation to run when you
want an activity that is calm and relaxing.
The participants follow a list of detailed
instructions closely, so it becomes more
about concentration and precision.

Here is an example of how it can be run
to spell the word 'Hello'.

Draw the first letter of your name.

Swap places.

Draw the second letter of your surname.

From now on, the letter instructions called
out will form a specific word, so it's
essential to keep this a secret by calling
out other instructions that deliberately
put the participants off the scent (such as
letters that don't form part of the word and
punctuation marks or pictures).

Draw an H.

Keep swapping places after each new instruction.

Draw a smile ...

An exclamation mark ...

Any letter you fancy!

Draw an E next to an H ...

A smile!

An L after an E ...

A sun ...

An L next to another L ...

A circle ...

An O after an L ...

Another exclamation mark!

Suddenly the word 'hello' – or whichever
word you've chosen – appears in many places
across page.

The letters may not be in the right order, but
that's not what's most important. Not only is
this fun as a game, the jumble of letters and
signs is also graphically pleasing.

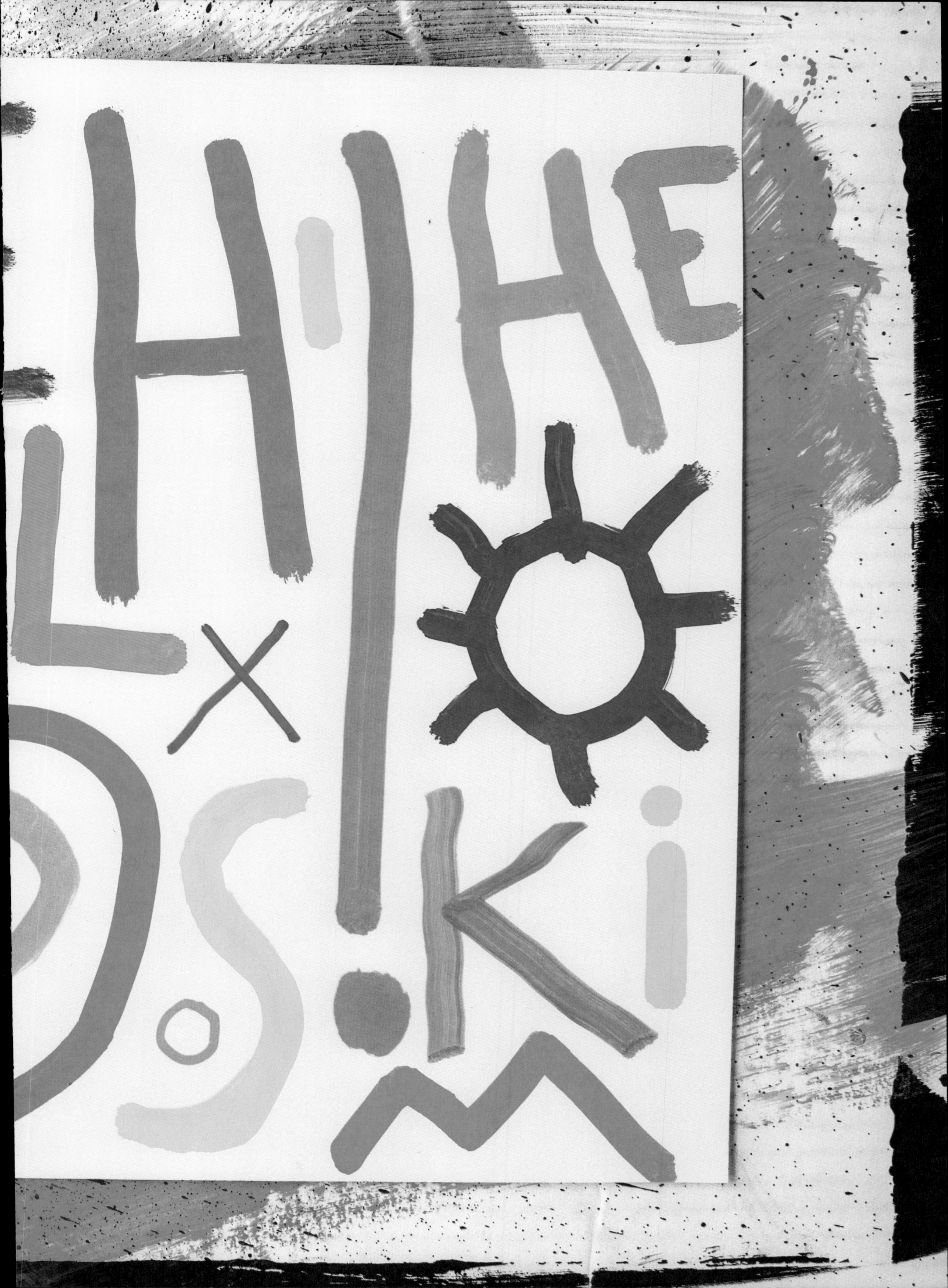

WHO'S THE FASTEST?

In this game your artists have to draw and pass their paper on to a neighbour at great speed, forcing them to improvise, be spontaneous and use visual shortcuts. As the game develops, I pick out interesting imagery and direct the group towards a joint composition. I like this game, because it is often the accidental marks and unexpected combinations that bring the most interesting results!

GETTING READY

A classroom is an ideal space because you can set your chairs and tables in a line without much trouble, but you can easily adapt this to any room. You'll need lots of A4 or letter size paper and some tape to fix the paper to the wall.

Take two pieces of paper, and place one at each end of the group. Everybody has pencils or pens in front of them.

THE WORKSHOP

You're each going to draw a shape on the pieces of paper. There are two pieces of paper, so you will need to think of two shapes to draw.

When the paper reaches you, draw your shape very quickly and pass it on to your neighbour.

You have 22 seconds for the pieces of paper to travel from one end to the other.

(You can, of course, adjust your timings according to your number of artists and their abilities.)

Ready, steady, go!

When the sheets have reached each end for the first time, I collect them and comment on them, jokily pretending to be cross: 'Come on everybody, couldn't we do better than these scribbles?' Then I tape the first sheets up on the board as visual reminders.

Close your eyes and think about the next shape you're going to draw on each piece of paper.

You have 30 seconds this time. Ready, steady, go!

Fresh pieces of paper are on the move.

This second round might not produce anything particularly clear, but I can usually pick out one or two interesting shapes. **'Ooh, something interesting happened this time!'** I highlight these, circling them and taping them to the wall, or drawing them on the board. It goes without saying that this is all very subjective, so you have to be interpretive and use your imagination!

GOOD

GREAT!

Pretty good, but I think we can do better!

Come on, let's start again! You have 50 seconds.

Now I take a closer look, pointing out which drawings interact with each other on the page, commenting on how one picture might create a visual dialogue with another. For example, one shape might look like a sun, and another like a tree – it could be the beginning of a scene!

←YES!

I give the participants more time for each round and continue to encourage the artists and choose interesting elements, which are circled and pinned up for everyone to remember so that they can re-use them or be inspired by them for the next round.

←YEAH!

After several rounds, the participants have created a group composition out of all the interesting elements recorded, which can then be used to make a bigger group painting (a fresco, for example) with poster paints, or to create a series of individual pictures, where each participant re-draws the communal composition in their own way.

By the end, the participants have created a group composition that they can be proud of.

VARiATioNS

Again at speed, the participants draw a pictogram that's more specific (house, wave, person etc.) each time the paper is passed.

THE GREAT SUMO MATCH

A wrestling match that ends in a feast? Why not? The title of this workshop is a trick to make our artists focus on the process, have fun and forget about the result, which is platefuls of delicious illustrations!

GETTING READY

Lay out sheets of paper – small, medium or big. Draw a large black circle on each piece of paper that takes up roughly half to two-thirds of the space.

Give each artist a different colour paint-cup (no black paint for Part One) and a paintbrush. Sit them in pairs opposite one another, across the paper. Prepare some black paint and brushes for Part Two.

THE WORKSHOP

PART ONE

Have you watched a sumo wrestling match before?

(You may need to explain how it works!)

Well, this is similar: you have to push your opponent out of the circle. Let's have some fun!

Dip your paintbrush in the paint and put it in the middle of the circle. When I say 'go', use your paintbrush to push your opponent's brush out of the circle. You must keep your paintbrush on the paper at all times.

Ready? Round One. Go!

Once an opponent's paintbrush is outside the circle, the round stops. I wait until everyone has finished, then ask them to swap pot and paintbrush with their neighbour.

Let's start again. Round Two. Go!

In general, I don't need to do this more than twice.

 P A R T T W O

Now we're going to make a meal! In front of you is a plate and you're going to draw a fork, a knife and a glass around it.

Let's prepare some delicious food. What are you going to treat yourself to? Look at the colours on your plate, then draw on top of them to make your dinner!

A simple line, squiggle or dot might be all it takes to conjure up fish, chicken, or even a salad. It's helpful to choose a different colour that's going to stand out for this bit, and black is a good choice.

The plates fill up in a few brushstrokes, and the food looks very tasty!

You've got some space left: decorate the tablecloth! And don't forget to fill your glass!

And finally, what are you going to call your delicious dish?

Bon appétit!

VARIATIONS

Sculpture: you could do the sumo match on paper plates. Then paint a tablecloth – either a real paper one, or lots of pieces of paper joined together, and stick the plates on to it. Add some disposable cups, knives and forks, *et voilá*! A 3-D meal that's good enough to eat!

A BODY OF WORK

This workshop aims to change the way we look at shapes through shifting our focus and perspective. By decorating unexpected areas of a larger silhouette, a striking group portrait is produced in a way that is accessible, fun and hugely rewarding.

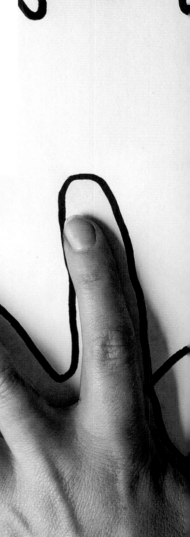

GETTING READY

Spread out some big sheets or rolls of paper, either on the floor or taped to the wall (in which case you'll also need a few chairs or stools).

First, lay out some thick pens, and have pots of different colour poster paints, crayons or chalk ready for afterwards.

THE WORKSHOP

PART ONE

Without saying a word, I choose one of the artists, position them against the paper and draw around their outline.

The audience is intrigued! Next, I draw around another of my participants with their arms and legs outstretched or in a dance position of their choice. I continue drawing more silhouettes, with lines and shapes overlapping, and once I have demonstrated what to do, I encourage my artists to join in!

Everybody, start drawing your friends' outlines!

Then, once the picture looks full enough ...

PART TWO

Now you're going to colour in only the places where your silhouettes overlap.

The children pick up their paint pots and concentrate solely on these intersections. As they apply the paint they forget about the original outlines and gradually transform the overall picture into planes of colour or even patterned zones. Once the intersections are

done, the artists can paint the background
and other empty areas too.

**Hey presto! The magic of colour means that
we're looking at the silhouettes in a completely
new way!**

**We've made a group portrait — colourful, cheerful
and as dynamic as a dance.**

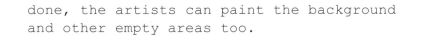

VARIATIONS

Shrink it down: instead of tracing the
outline of the whole body, you can just
draw around one part of it (for instance
intersections of hands or arms).

Create new themes: you can also draw around
objects in the classroom (exercise books,
biros, satchels), in the garden (pots,
spades, rakes), in the kitchen (glasses,
forks, grater), in the bathroom (bottles,
hair-dryer), in the play room or bedroom
(hoops, cushions), etc.

THE Big FEAST

This workshop always makes me hungry!
Together, we lay a banqueting table,
and add a feast of colours using all
kinds of household implements – with
mouthwatering results!

GETTING READY

Hang a large white canvas (this can be paper or fabric) on the wall, or spread it out on the floor: we're going to create a big, group drawing.

You'll need Indian ink and brushes for each participant, as well as cups of coloured poster paint and a set of separate paintbrushes.

You'll also need a big tub of assorted plastic implements: knives, forks, cookie cutters, empty vitamin tubes, combs, flyswatters or toothbrushes. Anything you can lay your hands on that might be useful for dipping in paint and making marks.

To begin, each participant has his or her own pot of ink and a brush.

THE WORKSHOP

PART ONE

Who'd like to dig into a feast? Let's start by laying the table! Pick up your brushes and dip them in the ink.

I encourage the artists to move around and draw in place settings here and there in ink to fill the table.

Don't forget, for our feast we need: plates, forks, knives, spoons, glasses, jugs, candlesticks, napkins and vases with flowers.

Once the paper is full ...

STOP
Stop, wait, let's see what we've achieved so far.

While the tablecloth is drying, the children have a break. During this pause, I lay out the plastic implements, cups of poster paint and paintbrushes.

PART TWO

Now, what would you like to eat? Let's fill our plates!

Next I encourage my artists to use their plastic
implements imaginatively! We dip the vitamin
tubes in the poster paints to make rings on
the plates; smear the flyswatters and splat them
on the plates; dip the comb and make grooves.
I keep the pace nice and calm so the different
elements don't get all mixed up on the plates.
If the colours do become so thick that they
clump together, I encourage intaglio: etching
shapes into the paint with a pointed implement
(a plastic knife, or even the tip of the
paintbrush handle).

Then, when the plates are full ...

And what are we going to drink?
We need to fill up the jugs.
Shall we have some bubbles in our glasses?

Now let's decorate the tablecloth.

The children pick up the cups of poster paint
and paintbrushes to draw splotches, crosses,
dots ... or we might even decide together on
a single design.

Nothing missing?
Look at our splendid banquet table, filled with
delicious-looking plates and yummy colours! Good
enough to eat!

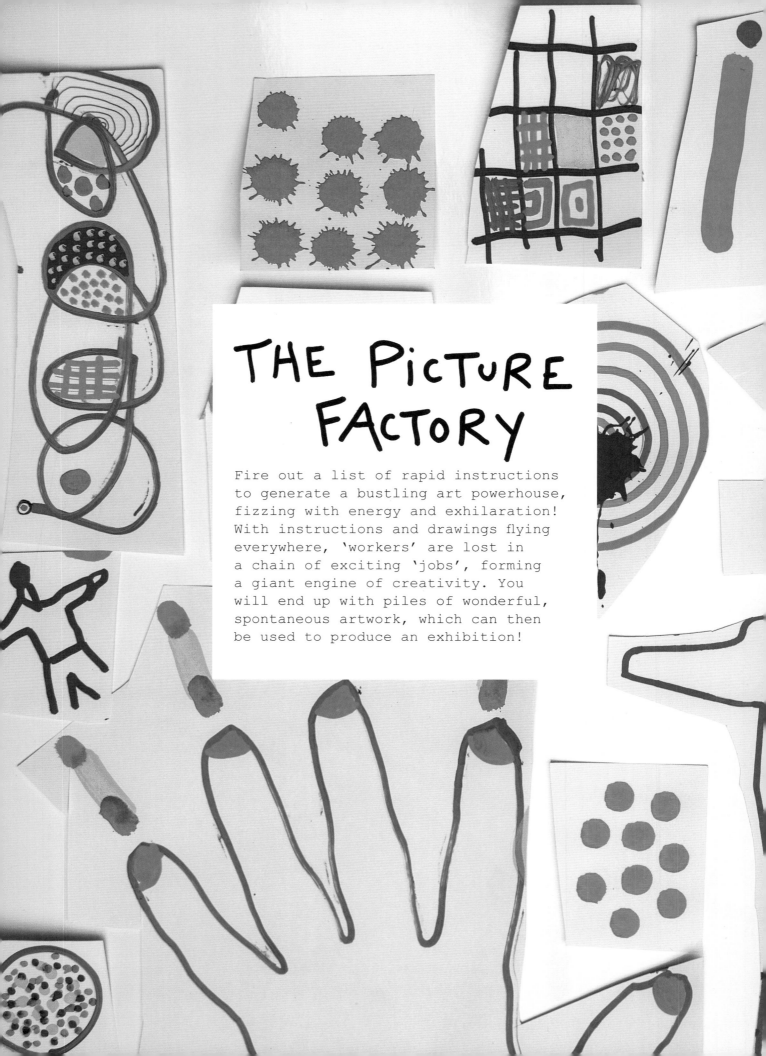

THE PICTURE FACTORY

Fire out a list of rapid instructions to generate a bustling art powerhouse, fizzing with energy and exhilaration! With instructions and drawings flying everywhere, 'workers' are lost in a chain of exciting 'jobs', forming a giant engine of creativity. You will end up with piles of wonderful, spontaneous artwork, which can then be used to produce an exhibition!

GETTING READY

You'll need enough space to allow small groups of 2-4 children to work around each other. Each group needs one sheet of paper (or whichever material you are using – see 'variations' below). Each group also needs several pots of different colour paint and paintbrushes or colouring pencils. Maybe prepare some lively music to get the 'workers' excited.

The idea of the Picture Factory is to create spontaneity by issuing rapid instructions to each group in turn. Instructions should be deliberately vague, leaving room for interpretation. The participants don't need to carry them out to the letter, but they do need to generate energy as a group. If the children ask 'Are we doing it right?', just give them more instructions!

THE WORKSHOP

I am the foreman, wandering around the factory floor. I point at groups in turn, issuing orders.

Dot, dot, dots everywhere. And lots of colours!

or

**I want circles around circles, around circles.
Then I want circles inside circles.**

or

Stripes, lines, lines, lines. Lines that get tangled up.

or

I want a giant doodle.

or

What do you want to draw? A tree? All right, but imagine you're in the tree.

Draw a circle, then another circle and another circle.
Then throw the paintbrush as if it's an arrow.

or

Draw a cloud. And after that I'd like a rainfall
of colours.

or

Trace the outlines of the objects I'm going to give you
and paint them.

or

Make some dots, then link the dots with lines.

or

Shapes, shapes, lots of different shapes! And no two
the same, okay?

or

Draw clouds in every colour.

or

Your job is to draw; and *your* job is to scribble on top of
his drawing.

or

Your job is to draw; and *your* job is to move the paper
while she draws.

Or

Draw with your eyes closed.

or

Tilt your paper and make your paint run.

OR

Draw a splotch on your paper, then stick it to another sheet of paper before it dries.

or

Draw some letters, numbers and exclamation marks.

And when you've finished, come back to see me!

When they come back, I issue fresh instructions to help them fine-tune and finish off their drawing, ensuring that the composition is as rich as possible:

Add dots/spots on dots/spots, marks or lines.

You can use some of the instructions from the other workshops if you like, or just make up your own. There are endless possibilities – just keep feeding the group's spontaneity, enthusiasm and energy!

When a page is full, I take it away and hand out a fresh sheet. Participants come to me, or I walk around to keep them moving, creating excitement, firing instructions and handing out paper. The goal is to get them lost in the moment. Result? A factory buzzing with enthusiastic workers who have shared a great moment together, and are surrounded by a mass of intuitive drawings.

Well done workers, you've produced some fantastic pictures today. Time to clock out!

VARiATioNS

Produce an exhibit: I've often run this workshop with the aim of displaying a final exhibition or a group sculpture. Turning a workshop into an exhibition is an ambitious project, which requires considerable experience and time (you can create it over several days or months), but by shifting gear from creating to displaying for others to look at, we achieve a lasting legacy, which is very rewarding for the participants.

If this is your aim, it's good to start the workshop itself with reasonably stiff shapes as canvases: card, cardboard or even plywood. This way, the works can be exhibited anywhere – on the floor, on the walls and even outside.

To transform these canvases into a collective sculpture, you'll need a system of notches to ensure they hold together. (Make the notches – two on each side – in the same place on all the shapes, with the same distance between notches).

You can often get stunning results if you prime all the media in the same way (with vibrant two-tone colour planes, one colour on each side).

Take a look at the photos of these sculptures at the end of this book – they should give you some ideas!

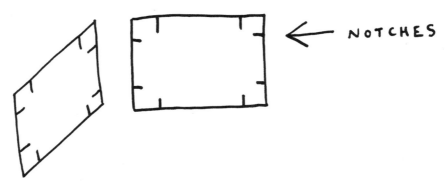

← NOTCHES

THE GREAT SPECTACLE

This is more than a workshop – it's a
spectacular show! The artists build
a picture through a pre-rehearsed,
choreographed performance, and as
the grand finale they reveal their
masterpiece. Wonderful!

GETTING READY

The working surface needs to be vertical: it could
be a wall, or sheets of paper hung up, rolls of
transparent paper (such as clear plastic for
covering books or acetate), a large, wooden fence, a
large window, etc.

The idea here is to create something choreoGRAPHIC;
a dance in which the participants become dynamic
painters, performing gestures that they've devised,
fine-tuned and rehearsed in the workshop.

For this workshop you'll need extra space to
run around.

And of course, music! These painters are also dancers!

Each participant knows exactly what to do, having
already rehearsed the group choreography. Here's
a scripted example of how the show might work.

THE WORKSHOP

Once the audience is settled in their seats,
let the music begin!

Our dancing painters arrive and draw a dot
or small circle. In another place, they draw
a square (rectangles are also fine).

Somewhere else they draw a vertical line,
somewhere else another square, somewhere
else a circle, and in another place a vertical
line. All of these marks can be at any angle or
position.

The dancers then mark a small circle or dot
above or below one of the squares.

Then they find a circle without a square,
and add a square above or below it.

Finally, they draw vertical lines out from the four corners of each of the squares.

We now have a series of dancing characters (refer to the image to see what I mean).

Still to the rhythm of the music, the participants now draw new, random shapes that interact and play with these dancers: marks indicating movement, bending, etc.

The audience will be surprised to see the composition coming together, revealing a dynamic picture full of the energy and movement that went into making it.

This is all about the performance: the excitement of moving to music, and creating a surprise picture live in front of an audience.

The great thing about this workshop is that the dancing figures are easy to assemble, easy to draw and immediately recognizable to the audience.

Now you know how it works, it's up to the Leader and the group to decide how to choreograph and rehearse the spectacle.

((((((VARiATiONS))))))

Anything goes: most of the workshops in this book could be transformed into live spectacles, by turning the ideas behind them into dynamic choreographies. With Portrait of a Word, for example, you could ask the painters to take it in turns drawing signs and letters in the jumble, which only make sense at the end of the choreography. Likewise, once the Flowers, Dice, Sumo or Traffic Jam workshops have been grasped and rehearsed by the group, there could be some fantastic staging of their pictures.

AND TO FINISH ...

When a workshop is over and there are cups of leftover paint, I think to myself, 'I should do something with those'.

I turn over a cup and whack it down on to the paper. I smear the shapes and colours. Huge splotches appear, which are great for drawing on. How about monsters or flowers or ...

What do you think? Over to you!

Hervé Tullet: Childhood Recaptured

An essay by Sophie Van der Linden

With over 70 publications to his name – all offering a beguiling blend of words, art and playfulness – Hervé Tullet has earned a loyal following from young enthusiasts the world over. And through his workshops he has built on that special connection in breathtaking ways.

Whether he's talking to a small group of schoolchildren in an African village, or to hundreds of participants and their families at a famous museum in Japan, Tullet's workshops always share the same hallmarks: an extraordinary creative energy unleashed in the participants and rigorously channelled by this experienced artist.

Once the materials are ready and the impatient participants are in position, the artist wanders barefoot among giant rolls of paper spread across the floor. He's relaxed but focused, alert to everything that's happening around him, with a sensory connection to both the group and the space.

Megaphone in hand, he calls out his directions to the group, who are drawn in by the rhythm of his voice and his witty and engaging instructions. His tall figure towers over his busy army of cheerful mini-creators. Initially they can be disoriented at having to swap places or move around, but this deliberate ploy by Tullet generates an energy and tension that stimulates excitement and creative play.

Tullet assumes the role of Children's General: mock-scary, but thoughtful and kind. To allow his participants free rein while also making clear demands of them is a rare combination, which explains what is so unique about the artist's talent. The same mix is also to be found in many of Tullet's books, which are full of explosive creative energy, bound in exquisitely realized volumes.

Constantly encouraged to keep moving, the children find themselves caught up in Tullet's creative effervescence. As music is introduced to sustain the rhythm, the young artists begin to speed up and images proliferate in every direction.

To those participants carried away by the excitement of drawing, Tullet gives subtle signs that communicate: 'That's great, leave it just as it is.' For others who are more hesitant, he might sketch in an idea or shape that they can respond to. Above all, he stabilizes the activity, sustains the energy and grasps every eventuality – even 'accidents' such as paint spills – as an opportunity to create. He is alert and reactive, always striking the right balance between the synergy of the participants and the necessary harmony of the composition. And he does so while ensuring that his control is secondary to the creative energy of the group.

This role is far from easy, since it requires a huge amount of concentration. The artist explains the experience by quoting jazz musician Martial Solal: 'You feel like you're falling, but you never fall.' Tullet likes to walk the wire in his workshops and court risk because he knows that the experience of creative collaboration will reward every participant and result in an original artwork that is special to them. Original, simply because the artworks created through these workshops don't rely on preconceived diagrams or a specific technique.

Above all, these activities shake up traditional ideas about a picture being 'well drawn'. By validating the splotch and the scribble, Tullet challenges the age-old notion that it takes a particular talent to produce art, he demonstrates that creativity evolves from our way of looking. Each exercise encourages children to look with fresh eyes and to appreciate what they produce, thereby getting rid of any hang-ups about artistic practice and skill. By supporting thousands of children in accomplishing something creative – based on a playful rather than a painstaking approach – Tullet really is performing a great public service.

Tullet's work invites children to a place where play is king; the kind of play envisaged by Bruno Munari – the great Italian artist and designer – who dedicated the end of his career to creating delightful, interactive books for children. Inspired by the same values as Munari, Tullet has embarked on a journey in the opposite direction, from children's illustrator to the artist. He perfectly embodies the poet Charles Baudelaire's wonderful theory: 'Genius is nothing more or less than childhood recaptured at will.'

Towards the end of the session, the artist gently begins to remove paintbrushes from hands, channelling the group energy towards a state of calm. It's all about recognizing when to stop work on a picture, to avoid it becoming muddled, without limiting the dynamism of the participants. The children take a few steps backwards. They can scarcely believe their eyes as they contemplate what they've made, whether it's a gigantic field of flowers or a beautiful, graphic portrait. As if by magic, the creative energy of the group has allowed each of them, without exception, to play a part in creating something wonderful.

A few children – who might be modest or reserved, but still very proud of what they've achieved – are so thrilled by the experience that they are determined to take their leave of the workshop leader. They go to shake his hand, or say 'thank you', in a happy, fulfilled whisper. Such moments of grace speak volumes about the impact of this artist like no other.

Sophie Van der Linden is a leading author, editor and critic of children's literature. She writes widely on children's publishing and picture books, lectures at Universities around Europe and also judges prestigious illustration competitions, such as the International Award for Illustration at the Bologna Children's Book Fair.

To Marie Da Silva and Luc Deschamps at the Jacaranda School for Orphans in Malawi, for their work and passion for children.

PHAIDON PRESS LTD
Regent's Wharf
All Saints Street
London N1 9PA

PHAIDON PRESS INC
65 Bleecker Street
New York, NY 10012

www.phaidon.com

First published 2015
© 2015 Phaidon Press Limited

ISBN 978 0 7148 6973 5

A CIP catalogue record for this book is available from the British Library.

Photos on p68 (4th and 6th clockwise from top left), courtesy of Electa

Project Editors:
Maya Gartner and
Hélène Gallois-Montbrun

Production Controller:
Adela Cory

Design:
Melanie Mues

Photographs:
Jake Green

Text written in collaboration with
Sophie Van der Linden

Translation:
Sarah Ardizzone

Printed in China

For more information about the author and his workshops, visit

www. herve-tullet .com

Children and safety: This book and the workshops presented in it have been designed for parents and childminders to run with children and assume adult supervision at all times. Children's abilities vary by age and by child, and although we take care to identify any hazards, we do not take any responsibility for your children during these activities. It is up to parents and childminders to choose age-appropriate materials and to ensure the safety of the children under their supervision.